A Short Collection of Sonnets

Charlie Standen

BookLeaf
Publishing

Presentation by *BookLeaf Publishing*

Web: www.bookleafpub.com

E-mail: info@bookleafpub.com

ISBN: 9789395026758

First edition 2022

DEDICATION

For Doris.

The Young Man's Call to Morning

'Your sharp air prizes open fog-struck eye,
Birdsong and faint engine assure the ear,
That all in night did not turn o'er and die,
And leave me, sole man, to the morning clear.

Candelabra of branch and grass of silver,
How oft have poets taken you for Muse?
You make mind blank, and unto it deliver,
High and noble thoughts that ignite and fuse.

You call upon the timeless voice within,
That one cannot reach through hard exertion,
Nor practice, nor patience, nor glug of gin,
Without thee I am but thoughtless urchin.

As I crunch along morning's lawn quiet,
Inspire my soul to revel and riot.'

The Frustrated Youth

'Here come dull thoughts, bright lights, and
heavy head,
Silence rings through with importunate whir,
Decayèd mind of intuition dead,
Look how I waste, a cantankerous cur.

Of wingèd things on high, I cannot think,
Caught in the cumbrous embrace of Comfort,
In her fat and milky arms so I slink,
And sleep hard with dreams of days triumphant.

Oh slit thine wrists, tedious Frailty,
Why must you temper mine poor spirit so?
With grossest grin, you hand treats so tasty,
Only to laugh on my hopeless sorrow.

So when I return with life force in full,
I will revenge myself in fashion cruel.'

On Curiosity

Man is creature curious of all things,
Pursuit of mystery is the sole cure,
Till we turn supine with now clippèd wings,
Sold death by life with mind still wanting more.

What is most fey and promises delight?
The love of one at the expense of all,
That spurs and smites all sides with giddied
fright,
The object is but change: a rise and fall.

The sea churnèd by wind misses its peace,
The pond gives its hand to Charybdis,
Neither in their toilings do ever cease,
Blinded by the tongues of Whisper and Hiss.

How can one calm, or of just fears allay,
But blindly teach to laugh, as did Rabelais?

The River under Lethe

Let love put boot unto your neck and find,
The land of those in wait for the Other,
Wat'ry eyes stare into the river blind,
In hopeless wait for the absent lover.

Some cannot swim but jump in all the same,
Their glassy eyes look to the azure sky,
Some thrash, some laugh, some sink under in
shame,
All to that sky alone make their goodbye.

I cannot say if they do right or wrong,
Only that my Self resists to follow.
But how beautiful are this hapless throng,
In crystal flow as but perch for swallow.

Oh noble souls with skin all cut and red,
Perhaps I'll join you before I'm dead.

The Hopeful Youth

5

'In night I wait with pen at the ready,
Fit to pounce upon any thought worthwhile,
Beleaguered by silence: whole and heavy,
Still seated I smirk with silent smile.

So aid me now fickle Other of mine,
Hand me freshest truths upon which to gorge,
And guzzle fast as Tempranillo wine,
And like Vulcan upon this page I'll forge.

I seek you not for trophy or laurel,
In your voice I take my sweetest delight,
My mind is placid and without quarrel,
Cultivate it rich with crop of great height.

Patience is the surest invocation,
As you near, I swell round with elation.'

The Budding of the Neurotic

From premature peak I do not stop and look,
To survey the past in all its glory,
It does not wink up from low-lying brook,
But is caught in the wind and sighs sorely.

Oh gradient of my mind's artifice,
That kept me sure of right path I did run,
Now gone and so left me wrenchèd from bliss,
To spin and dive, not knowing where the sun.

Yet life-juice does pulsate my ev'ry vein,
We were not born to understand at all,
Better suited to the anarchic reign,
Of formless Chaos and his empty hall.

And so with grin ecstatic I do race,
From room to room, nay better, place to place!

Lust

I was a slave, at your idol I knelt,
And gazed on your form in all its glory,
Lust did stab with its knife so sorely felt,
My ribs did pop with blood red and gory,

Your sable tresses atop the clear sea,
Your supple body sandlicked by the beach,
Your thick scent piquing all sensual glee,
Your softened thigh downed as the fresh-ripe
peach.

'Twas both our natures that led us to bed,
No conspiracy nor machination,
And that we failed to break free from fate's
thread,
Left us in this state of detestation.

To follow lust is no easy pursuit,
Harden your heart: for it faces a brute.

He Who Cannot See

'Mine bulging eyes do sag in their sockets,
Quite ready to splat wet upon the page,
The slow hand scratches out crawling sonnets,
Fit to no audience of any age.

Once roaring fires fade now to ebb and ash,
Viscous treacle replaces once hot blood,
A hollow shell painted bold gold and brash,
Fit but to stew in the sub-surface mud.

My bastard will is as a child at fare,
With fretting pace it runs from ride to ride,
And rushing fast as if no time to spare,
Sick of the choice; unable to decide.

In crooked ball I might well crawl up tight,
And let Life pass as through a gruesome night.'

Messian Straits

9

Quickly across the churning white-veined sea,
Go the sailors of the blue-prowèd ship,
Adjacent to Charybdis' sole tree,
As hanging caverns fall and headlands rip.

And there Ulysses stands before the mast,
Banishing the shrill wind with force of voice,
Wrenching the helm from spewing maelstrom
vast,
Cursing the Earthshaker with few words choice.

Yet have not his salty limbs gone rigid?
Why shift his grey-blue eyes from cave to cave?
As if aware of some omen wicked,
That swears to send six to a deepest grave.

Out echoes a shriek of most sick'ning pitch,
Prey to brine-toothed Scylla: unfortunate six!

Night

I swear by the light, it troubles me not,
Praise unto day and its steel structure strong,
I owe to it work and freedom from thought,
That ensnares me tight and holds on too long.

For such thoughts dwell in the alcoves of night,
Where Chaos reigns and banshees shriek their
tune,
Intangible and quick to avoid sight,
Swift tailors work unto the Devil's boon.

Clothes not they make but rather dreams of
sorts,
Embroidered by rent and mangled fingers,
Fit to unearth man's weak mind and distort,
It's life-vision till such doth not linger.

Here come the slow chills that jelly my spine,
As night swallows day and all things benign.

The Wonders of the Club

Paroxysms of sheer ecstasy,
Sharply revive my often deadchill core,
And the Now supercedes all fantasy,
A Now I covet until evermore.

A Swedish woman with a cigarette,
And an angled face and a square-toothed smile,
In the smoke one sees but a silhouette,
A glint of tooth and a vinyl pile.

From behind her the music resonates,
The music she roughly moulds as she might,
Forcing of me a shiver that full sates,
All shapes and forms of pleasure and delight.

Be there a purer form of hedonism,
Since those times known as Eleusinian?

On a Hill Above Truro

As clouds pass by in linear current,
Crows whirl as black plastic bags caught in
storm,
Grass bends and screams in pitch abhorrent,
All moves, all is spontaneous in form.

A wren in knife-edge lattice doth shelter,
And maelstrom ubiquitous howls the more,
Indoors alike stay both young and elder,
As my lips turn'd carmite, parch-dry, and raw.

In this basin of once verdant pasture,
Lies mass of crumble-stone and shatter-slate,
More dead in hue than those on Charon's shore,
No right to restoration or new fate.

An ebb of prosperity and, once, pride,
A speck upon the Fal: I watched you die.

The Ambitious Youth

'In vaguest future lies uncertain path,
Numerous ends appeal to me alike,
Though I settle not for fulfillment half,
Fruit of Destiny: I shall pluck thee ripe.

Still I wish to pursue all endeavour,
To strive with athletes, poets, all the more,
Yet I cannot compete in equal measure,
Thanks to Fortune: Nature's most poison whore.

With zeal of criminal, I labour on,
For light of day is naught without one's will,
With coilèd limb ready to pounce upon,
Those bones of Fortune in which lie my fill.

You who have been upon the path barefoot,
Show me the way and first step where to put.'

The Contented Observer

'Thou art a constant hive of bustle and fuss,
In both thousand ways and none so you move,
As wand'ring eye I watch with slowèd pulse,
Within your storm I find balm which to soothe.

High praise to invisibility,
With right to observe in clime calm and still,
My eyes admire, free of lubricity,
Setting matters not: be it town or hill.

Thus when I overlook such pleasures true,
Conscience be there to reprimand and chide,
For such time wasted be but mine to rue,
Relight my senses; keep open my eyes.

If Fortune were supplicant of desire,
Here I would sit o'er all places higher.

The Revelations of the Scholar

'With youthful vigour I pursued you far,
Yet with Mercury's boots, quick to evade,
I searched in Bible, Quran, Kabbalah,
But still you dodged my honest efforts made.

Perhaps frustrated I gave up the chase,
For truth can no longer my object be,
Too shy, too slippy, born of unknown race,
Instead I pledge my soul to you: Beauty.

Only Beauty can shake mine poisèd spine,
You are sole recipient of my tears,
In you are found the perfect and divine,
You are both ecstasy and wildest fear.

To you I pledge myself apprentice new,
Carve into me more noble attitude.

The Lies of the Wise

To make one's bed or clean one's sullied room,
Those wise sophists claim these the keys to life:
'Without strictest order one's bound for doom,
To the blackened beast you'll be bound as wife.

'Of days endless and nights ever the more,
To stew in hollow cell of thine own hand,
And take all aspect to eternal war,
Till soul is ground down to the deadest sand.'

Hark not to the call of these wheezing corpses,
Look how their sallow skin creeps with
maggots,
Elope from these and their sickly thorpes,
Free then to add bands to soul of agate.

Fast run to solitude and train your mind,
With spirit free to roam land, sea, or sky.

A Cautious Man's Ode to Future

'Such bliss do you promise upon the now,
With winkèd eye and smile lascivious,
Caress the hapless under shady bough,
And make mockery of the piteous.

Adages old warn against your foul ways,
As you conspire with closest twin (Fortune),
And lead many down labyrinthine maze,
Where love counts for naught, nor faith, nor
caution.

In the present thus seek refuge secure,
And carve your way until next tomorrow,
Then when renewèd, repeat evermore,
Till poor Future cries out dole and sorrow.

Here all must place their eggs and their basket,
Leave plans and predictions unto the half-wits.'

A Youthful Uncertainty

What is that push that sends me down the path?
To consider it good is thought naive,
I know full well in me lies evil wrath,
With wetted lust to lie, to kill, to thieve.

Should from mine castle these thoughts be
banished?
But then I as I am would cease to be,
There are frail times when this has been my
wish:
To lie as passive wrack on lonely sea.

But my dear will collects me from the deep,
And so chastises me for such thinking,
With smarting smite, I wake from doleful weep,
Now with feet ashore, no longer sinking.

Who am I to dispute which way is right?
Better to be than mock from lofty height.

Black Thoughts

To Ducasse and Rimbaud I owe so much,
See the beauty of their dark tainted minds,
Their prose of thickest pitch the soul do touch,
And soon finds itself with theirs full entwined.

All in its core is highest perfection,
The pure silence, the blank slate of the soul,
Yet our senses fill us with dejection,
Both sights and sounds repugnant to behold.

Oh Maldoror, prophet of pure disgust,
Of life rebuff and to yourself retire,
Dispel false truths of love, faith, and the just,
Choose noble torment; wallow in the mire.

In your voice I detect the faintest tone,
That to me is the truth and that alone.

Toil

I can hear the blood pumping in my ears,
My eyes do squint and struggle in the dark,
In my stupor, the evil shadows sneer,
As blood licks at my teeth with stain and mark.

Why can I not simply continue on,
Why must weakness bring me to but a crawl,
Spirit ablaze in me once found now gone,
A husk of man that moans and weeps and bawls.

Noble thoughts are not born e'er for practice,
For man is frail and his mind grandiose,
Hope fights with the earth and all its blackness,
Only changing few shades to grey at most.

Perhaps in the whole there lies more hope,
Dragging each forward with timeless rope.

A Pious Pedlar With His Sack

Alongside algaed brook and o'er vale,
Trundles a swarthy pedlar with his sack,
Oh poor Atlas! Sharp bent with back wrenched
frail,
Down with your goods and leave this cursèd
track.

Lie upon swarth as knights that did before,
Rub leathern cheek 'pon gossamer and dew,
Through swift rivulet drift your fingers sore,
And muse on the sky's ever-changing hue.

Oh suff'ring pedlar with thy mind unbound,
From divine Truth so unhappily torn,
Repulsed by endless Sight and grinding Sound,
Enclosed in Tophet-trap of razor thorn.

But swim, in the water such thoughts rush out,
Replace them new: dispell all doubt.

www.ingramcontent.com/pod-product-compliance
Lightning Source LLC
Chambersburg PA
CBHW070736160726
48003CB00006BA/2531